Product Pricing Strategies

15 Efficient and Effective methods to price your product

By John S. Burt

Legal Notice

The Distributor has strived to be all around as exact and finish as conceivable in the making of this report, despite the way that he warrants or addresses absolutely never that the items inside are precise because of the quickly changing nature of the Web.

While all endeavors have been made to check data given in this distribution, the Distributer takes care of blunders, exclusions, or opposite understanding of the topic thus. Any apparent affronts of explicit people, people groups, or associations are inadvertent.

In reasonable exhortation books, similar to whatever else throughout everyday life, there are no certifications of pay made. Perusers are forewarned to answer on their own judgment about their singular conditions to likewise act.

This book isn't planned for use as a wellspring of lawful, business, bookkeeping or monetary counsel. All perusers are educated to look for administrations with respect to able experts in lawful, business, bookkeeping, and money field.

You are urged to print this book for simple perusing.

Table of content

Estimating

Working with Buyers Who Are Price Aware Step by step instructions to Accomplish "Winning Cost"

Estimating As per the Kind of Item

Pricing Strategies That Increase Profitability

Value Skimming As an Evaluating Procedure

Is Mental Valuing a Powerful Methodology?

Market Entrance Estimating

Promotional Pricing

Competitive pricing

Offering discounts as a Piece of Your Estimating System

Elective Estimating Techniques

Change Costs to Make Your Contributions Really Engaging in Non-Value Ways

Esteem Based Estimating

How To Be Aware Assuming Your Evaluation Is Correct?

<u>Estimating</u>

Everything You Need to Know If you want to sell something online, the most crucial decision you will ever make is how to price your services or products. Since the Web gives a large number of options in contrast to the clients, you should be at standard with the opposition. The costs that you pay will decide how long you can remain on the lookout.

You really want to obtain an obvious thought regarding evaluating. How much could you at any point push it? How frequently do you have to survey the costs? A ton would rely on how you handle this phase of business. You need to pinpoint a purchaser gathering in the first place and afterward gauge the amount they might want to pay for your administrations or items.

In any case, other than that you additionally need to guarantee that you create some gain for yourself. What's more, regularly these two requests can be in struggle with one another. Various individuals utilize various strategies to set the costs of their items. Some of them have a logical premise and some don't. Given beneath is one such system which works with a comprehension of the creation cost, client assumptions and different players in the field.

Cost is characterized as the whole of the costs that you cause while making an item. Costs incorporate expense of natural substance, apparatus, bundling, conveyance and so forth. The amount that customers must pay for each unit of your product or service is its price.

For you to create a gain, the cost ought to be more than the expense. Your costs ought to be reliably over the expense in the event that you are wanting to run your organization for quite a while, besides in extraordinary cases. At times you can bring down the costs, to acquire passage into a business opportunity for instance. People would notice you if your prices were lower than your competitors'. Furthermore, when you gather a fair number of clients you can steadily increment costs!

How much would clients pay for your administrations is straightforwardly relative to how huge and significant they think your item is. Obviously your showcasing methodologies and notoriety in the market will assume a huge part in such a manner.

Between these two numbers, your expense and the value your clients will pay for your item lies your optimal cost. In the long run, it would definitely work in your favor if your price is a little lower than what your customers are willing to pay for your services.

Assuming your cost is higher than what is fair according to the client you would wind up losing your allure and market and bit by bit your feasibility.

Working with Buyers Who Are Price Aware

The stark reality of the value of money in today's world has made customers who are shopping for their needs more aware of the cash factor.

They hope that benefiting from the least cash spent to that end, evaluating your items accurately goes far in guaranteeing that you continue to get clients and create gains. In any case, that fundamentally doesn't imply that you can charm your clients by lessening costs, as this can frequently prompt misfortunes.

However, more than value, the worth of the item decides its cost according to the client. One won't ever expect a high profile vehicle like a Mercedes to be valued as per the pace of a Toyota, yet they will hope to get the best arrangement from you while looking to purchase a Toyota on the lookout.

Hence increasing the value of any item through great promoting, innovative work is a certain short approach to guaranteeing your client appreciating and consenting to the cost and the value of the item. In this way it is a straightforward truth of changing how the client checks an item out.

The easiest and productive technique to fulfill a cost delicate purchaser is to provide them with a striking image of the advantages this spending will get them over the long haul. Everyone likes to realize that they spent great cash on something that will endure and bring back additional profits. So in the event that you can persuade the client that purchasing something isn't just about spending yet putting resources into something advantageous and long haul, they will consent to spend the cash.

Showing how the more costly item will in the end lead to lesser issues and subsequently save a ton of problems and pointless spending on overhauling and fixes, you may simply have the option to secure the arrangement. This is again about persuading their clients they are doing the astute thing in checking out at the drawn out advantages of the buy.

On the off chance that you have a quality item and market it well any rational client will come to you. Regardless of whether it implies spending that additional buck, clients need the best on the lookout for themselves. So giving quality items never flops in bringing back clients for more.

Prevailing upon cost delicate purchasers requires understanding that cost isn't the main part of their purchasing choices. You will be able to demonstrate the full value of your service or customer when you take the time to learn about their requirements. Assuming you neglect to reveal the total picture you might wind up in the place of noting cost concerns, and over the long haul that won't assist your business with succeeding.

So know your clients. Sort out how their brains work and what they need. This will go quite far in persuading and charming them to purchase the right, despite the fact that it is a costly item. On the off chance that you neglect to comprehend that purchasing isn't just about the cash, however the wide range of various things referenced above, you would need to continue to diminish costs to get clients and that won't be too productive to your business.

Step by step instructions to Accomplish "Winning Cost"

Setting a cost for your item or administrations, particularly when you are attempting to sell on the Web, can be the most significant business choice. Setting a cost isn't quite so basic as it would sound. Assuming that you are hoping to create gain your cost ought to be more than your expense yet it must be lower than the 'value the market can bear', for example the value your clients hope to pay for your administration. You need to remember these things while valuing your items.

There are intricate estimating plans that you ought to comprehend and have the option to work with. What valuing plan you need to work with would rely upon your plan of action.

Like the 'Valuing to Enter' plan. This plan would work for you assuming your point is to infiltrate the objective market, rapidly. Your product's price must be low in order to achieve this goal.

Be that as it may, it's essential to conclude how low you can do without stirring things up around town. You really want to sort out the most reduced you can do without running into obligations and weighty misfortunes. You shouldn't have misgivings about causing starting misfortunes assuming you will receive long haul clients consequently.

Yet, how would you decide the lifetime worth of any client?

Secure in your normal clients and ensure you go to lengths to make them adhere to your specific image. Entrance evaluation is valuable in the event that you will establish a durable connection. It can likewise be valuable in conditions where a ton of new players are bouncing into the market.

Your item ought to be a definitive 'tacky item' which the client can relinquish. Online dealers for instance, are a lot more helpful that once snared individuals don't even for one second consider choices.

One more method for guaranteeing that the client returns is to make an outstanding item. While selling books online for instance, an extraordinary book with a decent cost would guarantee your moment of prominence.

Amazon.com for instance is the main player among online book shops on account of their vigorously sponsored rates. Despite the fact that this business strategy could have cost them numerous 1,000 bucks however they have figured out how to make a strong client base which they can now bank upon.

One more practical model, in actuality, is the way organizations that produce razors hit upon the possibility that it would be significantly more productive to exchange disposable cutters than handles, and the rest as is commonly said is history.

Finding the right cost for your item is the way to progress, in both the long and the present moment. The right cost for your item would lie somewhere close to the expense and the value a client is prepared to pay for your administrations. The expense would remember the costs for the unrefined components and other fixed and variable costs brought about in the assembling.

To such an extent, that it can likewise create your gains two times or threefold the current sum. Your items will actually can be categorized as one of the two classifications:

Commodity: There is a lot of contest in this field, on the grounds that the results of the various players in the field are the very it's just the value that they are contending on. You should be well honed and continually on your toes. The only things that would set you apart are your skill and efficiency. A little carelessness will wreck things in the future.

Appropriateness items: These are valid items. Authentic and unique in their own standing. You rival different players in the market on the strength of the exceptional qualities of your administrations. Assuming you are sufficient and popular you can set a value that you guarantee the best benefit for you.

The market on the Web is quickly evolving. To keep up you could need to modify your costs oftentimes, attributable to new contests and changes sought after and so on.

Then there are some products that are both commodity and proprietary, like computer hardware. PC frameworks are getting continually updated and that's only the tip of the iceberg and more modern and the opposition is relentless. It's a respectable item as a Mac can in any case stand to be substantially more costly than an ordinary Windows framework due to the extra elements it offers.

At any rate, regardless of what you do, you can't stand to value your item wrongly on the grounds that it can mean a moment passing on the lookout.

Cost battles these days are a piece of regular presence for any association. To get by, you need to continually be on your toes and convey anything you guarantee. Everyone must lower their prices if even one competitor does so. However, if you won't, you should have ample justification to maintain your position. A solid client base which would stay with you come what may, can be one valid justification.

Pricing strategies are a component of the marketing mix that are frequently overlooked. They can generally affect benefit, so ought to be given similar thought as advancement and promoting systems. Both gross margins and sales volume can be significantly altered by raising or lowering the price. This by implication influences different costs by lessening stockpiling costs, for instance, or setting out open doors for volume limits with providers.

Your best pricing strategy is also determined by other factors. Think about the five powers that impact other business choices: your rivals, your providers, the accessibility of substitute items, and your clients. It's also important to think about how you want to be seen by your audience. Value a superior thing excessively low, for instance, and clients won't completely accept that the quality is sufficient. On the other hand, if you set the selling price of value lines too high, customers will buy items at lower prices from competitors.

Some estimating procedures to consider are:

Cutthroat valuing

Holding your costs corresponding to your rivals is the most ideal way to carry on with work. Remain alert about how much your nearby rival is evaluating their items and afterward value yours comparable or lesser to theirs.

Cost in addition to increase

The total converse of the past method of strategies, this targets fixing your costs as indicated by your desire, according to the additional percent you need to keep and not the market. Yet, similarly as this enjoys the benefit of acquiring your parts through setting modest costs, this may likewise work antagonistically under particular conditions. So think and choose carefully prior to setting the cost.

Misfortune Pioneer

One more viable technique to charm clients and raise deals extensively is to sell somewhat modest things at a lower cost to clients who can possibly purchase more costly things. Be that as it may, this is a generally impermanent plan and can frequently end up being a bet.

Close out

This is an intriguing strategy to attempt when you are getting out your stock. This technique includes selling your additional merchandise at very modest rates all together forestall misfortunes.

Enrollment or exchange limiting

Know your clients. Short rundown the ones who can harvest your benefits and give them unique offers with the goal that they wind up getting charmed into purchasing more from you and furthermore make you want more. So decrease costs, give limits, take the necessary steps to get them back into your shop.

Packaging and amount limits.

The straightforward one in addition to one free likewise works perfectly. So give select clients a significant markdown on mass buys, both of similar kind, as in 5 shirts, or comparable or related things. Also, to stay away from misfortunes, put offers in old stock or group up one new with old to get out overabundance products.

Forming

Putting various variants of a similar fundamental item and afterward offering lower costs for the more essential models is a decent way to not just dispose of those models to average individuals. Yet, one can likewise collaborate offers like free overhauling for a period with the more expensive ones to fill in as motivator for the high buying clients.

So feel free to utilize these strategies to get the degree of benefit you've generally wanted.

Of all the promoting procedures you will use in your business, the valuing methodology is one of the most significant. Alongside picking the right item, insightful promoting, and a sound deals plan the right value procedure will decide your incomes and piece of the pie. Generally the forerunners in their industry use market skimming as an estimating strategy.

A computer manufacturer's plan is to release a new laptop about every eight months. He brings down the cost of the more established, unsold models (in their developing stage) and keeps the cost of the new workstations (in their starting stage) higher. The new workstations will request a greater cost based on their more up to date includes.

So the producer is skimming the cost (or skimming the market) at various stages - initial, development, development and decline. He acquires the most extreme benefit through the greatest cost that every one of these stages order.

A company with a low cost structure and a sufficient number of buyers will benefit from this strategy in a large market. In the above model with workstations, the interest is high, there are a lot of repeating purchasers with an industry which has a minimal expense structure that is innovation empowered.

Presently the test for the organization comes from the way that there are a lot of rivals in this market. In the event that these contenders have a full line of comparable items each with a shifting life cycle, purchasers will find it very hard to pass judgment on the item regarding its quality or administration or the incentive for cost.

Confronted with a flood of comparative looking items the purchaser will pick a PC with most extreme highlights at the least cost. Furthermore, on the off chance that your organization isn't the one with the most minimal value it might hurt it's image notoriety for it will appear as though you have been overpricing items which will ultimately prompt a drop of deals.

Before any value technique is selected, guarantee that you first review the market cautiously. One ought to have a reasonable thought regarding the clients' way of behaving and the manner by which the contenders will act or respond. Furthermore, this methodology ought to persistently be tried while it is applied to guarantee that the variables which prompted this technique have not changed over the long run with changing economic situations.

Cost has a mental importance attached to it. Purchasers have this conviction that on the off chance that an item is profoundly estimated, it is more significant. Albeit this conviction is more mental than reality based it makes physical assets more compelling than the actual item.

Notwithstanding, it is intriguing that as the purchaser begins investigating the idea of the item to a greater extent his choices become more reasonable and greater cost fails to be the estimating bar for item esteem. One good illustration of psychological pricing is when consumers believe they are getting a better deal at prices that end in even numbers, like $20, $66, etc., rather than prices that end in even numbers, like $9, $99, etc.

 In the event that the items to be estimated are in a cost "band" as in web-based barters or on the other hand in the event that they are evaluated in an odd reach figures like $199,00, the items will be viewed as more significant than a $200,00 posting. The brain science behind such customer conduct is that costs in an odd reach are generally viewed as a superior deal. Consequently, it is essential to ensure that you have picked the right cost and the right methodology for the item.

One more occurrence of mental estimating is reference valuing. Reference estimating is the point at which the purchasers connect with a cost mentally since it straightforwardly mirrors their in regards to the relationship of an item to its cost. If there should arise an occurrence of high worth items, for example, extravagant things, reference estimating is exceptionally persuasive and a whole business can be gained by this premise.

Nonetheless, one must be cautious while situating the costs since the technique might blow up on the off chance that the purchaser feels that the item doesn't merit being in that class. Reference pricing is a good pricing strategy if the product has features that make it appealing to buyers who are sensitive to their egos.

An illustration of this is very good quality extravagance things which appeal to inner self delicate purchasers. You must ensure that the price you have set for a product fits it best from all angles, including your own, for reference pricing to be successful.

Guarantee that the choice cost fits the item and the cost has been tried before it is delivered into the objective market. The impact of different components of the market on the sticker price should likewise be thought of. The item should be good at a mental cost procedure, the limited time program ought to be sufficient for the estimating system and the dissemination directs ought to be in a state of harmony with the cost and not supersede the expense of the actual item.

A fast section cost methodology that assumes that deals volume rise when an item is evaluated low which lessens the general expenses is called market infiltration valuing. This is a valuable technique that can be utilized in cost touchy business sectors. For instance, think about the market for blu ray players; here deals volumes are high, yet the quantity of contenders is high also.

The creation expenses of blu ray players have fallen radically and continually advancing innovation has considered the fast presentation of new highlights and advantages on new models. The organizations that spend money on blu ray players and sell high volume at low or sensible costs are following a market infiltration methodology.

Business people utilizing market entrance evaluating for the most part attempt to grow a business opportunity for their image and in the process enter the market for the item in general. All estimations depend on the understanding that the most reduced cost will win the biggest portion of the market. However, before employing this pricing strategy, it is crucial to first assess your market, price sensitivity, and price elasticity or inelasticity.

A specific measure of statistical surveying is likewise important for you to comprehend and prejudge how your rivals will respond to this gg evaluating methodology. For instance, if your low price prompts your rival to do the same, it will end in failure because you will then lower your price again, prompting a similar reaction from him. This will continue, and no one will win.

While information exchanged before is valid, it is likewise a fact that your market entrance estimating system can only be a hindrance for new contenders who are thinking about entering the market. When they consider how low your price is, they will see that their margin will be low, so considering the risks, they might choose not to enter the market. The risk for a new entrant of getting a sizable market share is extremely high.

However, for you to find success with this methodology, you should be ready to partake in the economies of the scale that high deals volume will bring and be the minimal expense supplier on the lookout.

In the event that you have a current business and your rival is following a market entrance system, you need to do a similar exhaustive examination and assessment of the market and you own abilities:

Is it attainable for you to bring down your expenses? Can you guarantee that it will produce large quantities? Could you at any point face the challenge of selling your item at a low cost (and trust volume deals will get you the portion of the overall industry and the productivity you need?)

If you answered no to all of these questions, you should carefully consider this penetration strategy before implementing it, and if you are still unsure, you should not implement the strategy.

However, if you are a new business owner considering this strategy in a sparsely populated or new market with little competition, you should concentrate on ways to reduce costs and increase efficiency.

Regardless of the evaluating technique you choose to utilize, ensure that you determine it in your showcasing blend plan with the purposes behind your decision.

Assess your picked promoting technique remembering your valuing procedure basically for a yearly premise at the hour of your strategy update, and guarantee it is the right system for your item considering the economic situations and for your customers and rivals.

Promotional pricing is typically utilized during the launch of a new product. It is utilized to invigorate interest for those items which have a slacking interest. The cost target purchasers are normally the ones searching for the arrangement. A few instances of these limited time occasion evaluating are intended for extraordinary occasions. These are generally implied for specific occasions that could be Christmas or Easter.

There are refund projects or recompenses that are accessible while purchasing a home. In some cases the vendor offers a move in recompense or floor covering substitution or remodel remittance or a refund for all money with no issue with funding or buying of enormous things like vehicles. There are many stores that would promote no interest supporting credits for their furniture bought.

Vehicle sales center likewise offers these estimating programs for their earlier year models. These systems in the deals field have been extremely effective however while utilizing these procedures you must be cautious since clients are turning out to be more delicate to the genuine worth of the techniques. Another stage procedure that appears to work is get one get one free or get two for the cost of one.

This is conceivable assuming the item cost is low, with solid net revenue and furthermore in the event of over weight of stock. The extended payment term, a payment method, may also be an important mode.

You want to pay a store and pay throughout some stretch of time. You would have the option to get the item just when you settle up. This is extremely normal among the redesign and development industry as the installment is made first as the underlying expense, then when the venture is most of the way and later while it is finished.

At times the minimal expense guarantee or no charge helps in these business techniques. A decent item typically has no return and a client is persuaded. In this way these techniques yield a positive effect. The over utilization of these systems has prompted a client's distrust. They search for the truth in the arrangement. The most frequently utilized special evaluating is the " leaving business" deal.

This deal might be deceiving as it might misdirect. This is the same company moving. As a client you ought to know that you are not being hoodwinked into such a plan. There are as yet numerous viable special estimating programs, so be shrewd regarding how to foster your valuing techniques.

To sort out regardless of whether your things are valued excessively high, do what your client does. Search the web. As per 2006 yippee!/OMD, there are around 66% of families who utilize the Web to investigate an item and 64% utilize the web crawler to purchase an item.

Take any of your items and look into the Web. Contrast the costs and others, this would help you to sell more. It is straightforward, you simply have to type the name and request to look at costs. Depending on the product you sell and market saturation, it may take some time. This would give significant knowledge that would help your business and make you mindful of what you are facing.

You might have the option to separate your item and persuade your client so they purchase from you. Begin this by bringing down your expenses. This generally makes a difference. Assuming you see that there is a plausible additional bringing down your costs then, at that point, do as such. You would find that your thing will turn out to be "most minimal cost ever on the web!". Minimal expense helps buy and this would compensate for any shortfall of cost cut.

 Ensure a cost match. Tell your clients that you would match any cost and you won't be under-sold. When the clients are there, cause them to completely finish the buy. You could likewise offer them free shipment. If your product costs more than your rival's, you could offer free shipping so that customers would pay the least at checkout.

Free delivery adds as a reward to any buyer. This word has a gigantic effect whether you at long last make the deal. If by chance you free a client it would be a result of the client not persuaded by the expense of the thing. Therefore, it is essential to make a few adjustments in order to persuade your customers that your product is definitely worth the price and is worth purchasing from you.

Cost isn't the main variable however quite possibly of those most significant elements that impact buy. So in the event that you have given your client a best purchase if there should arise an occurrence of the item worth the effort would assist you with having an edge over the other contenders.

Estimating products is troublesome. No single determinant sorcery recipe exists that will choose the best value for one's item. There is no basic technique except for one can go to particular lengths to make more powerful valuing arrangements. It is hard to be sure about valuing choices, one can depend on one's own judgment. However, even when doing so, decisions never quite meet expectations.

The value assurance of labor and products is perhaps the most imperative one in business. The cost of items must be finished so that the planned clients will pay that sum and furthermore one that creates benefit for the organization or the business won't keep going long.

There are a few logical and non logical ways to deal with evaluating. Introduced underneath is a structure for settling on evaluating choices that considers your expenses, the impacts of the contest and the client's view of significant worth.

Pricing policies are often overlooked as part of marketing, but they can have a significant impact on profits and should be given the same consideration as advertising and promotion strategies. Variety in cost can significantly change both gross edges and deals volume. This prompts roundabout impacts on different costs by diminishing stockpiling costs, for example, or setting out open doors for volume limits with providers.

Your estimating procedure could consider rebate offers to shoppers who offer you a business advantage.

Discounts in cash may be offered to customers who pay immediately. This framework subsequently remunerates the people who assist one's organization with keeping a consistent, positive income and diminishing credit-assortment costs.

Amount limits for huge orders seem OK when the expense per-unit to sell or convey an item decreases as the amount increments. A food provider, for example, may take care of a request for 12 dozen cupcakes for one client at a dime each, while cupcakes sitting in the bread shop shoe rack might be offered to a few clients over the course of the day for 20 pennies each.

This is done because it is necessary to take into account the possibility that some of the cupcakes will not sell. Costs are likewise connected with keeping the store open for irregular clients' accommodation. There are expenses related to having the store open for irregular clients' comfort.

Occasional limits really reward clients who basically help an organization in adjusting its income and in fulfilling creation needs.

Exchange stipends for returned old merchandise that one may either re-use or exchange for a benefit benefits both an organization and customers.

Special remittances much of the time seem OK. For example, on the off chance that your item is utilized in promotion crusades or in special exercises by a corporate store that likewise sells your item it winds up giving influence to your showcasing endeavors. If this is the case, you might decide to give the retail chain that does this a discount on your price.

Estimating is positively one of the main elements of your promoting blend system. Right estimating can make your item a hit or a disappointment on the lookout. The elements that must be remembered when it are the accompanying to showcase your item:

It must be of predominant quality
It ought to have highlights that your purchasers require or want
It ought to be unique in relation to what your rivals bring to the table
It ought to have a decent expense structure
You ought to likewise focus on areas of strength for a mission
Remembering these elements, it is critical to decide the valuing methodology that assists you with effectively selling your item on the lookout.

Given beneath are some elective estimating procedures:

Conventional or Financial estimating: The buyer is enticed by the low price in this tactic. It's typical of low-end or generic brands. For this methodology to be productive, you ought to have a minimal expense structure, insignificant elements and advancement. At the same time, guarantee that you harvest a few strong, stable advantages.

Pricing differentiation: In this strategy, the thought is to set the value as per different purchaser types, (for example the cost will vary for a web-based store, a retail location and a departmental store); geological region, (costs can be higher in California than in Illinois); by the amount bought (an individual purchasing enormous amounts will get a rate not the same as one purchasing a little amount); based on public record fragment (the value charged to a public record will shift from that charged to a nearby record). Do recollect, there must be a legitimate justification for applying differential evaluating.

Premium valuing: This methodology is pertinent for extravagance or top of the line products, for example, costly adornments, yachts, planes, bequests and so on. You can utilize this procedure on the off chance that the market perceives your item as an extravagance or premium thing.

Pricing of companion products or captive products: This technique can be adjusted to product offering evaluation also. For this situation, items are packaged together as buddies and valued as needs be. (for example a blender and blending bowl). They additionally think about items as prisoners (for example a razor that must be fitted with a specific edge). These items are much of the time bundled in a solitary bundle. (for example sharp edges might be bundled with the razor) The costs of these items outside a bundle typically will generally be higher.

Make sure to survey your items cautiously prior to picking a specific procedure so the valuing is fitting.

The days when men depended on Gillette, and ladies didn't look past Guerlain are a distant memory. There are seldom any imposing business models on the planet market, and each item in the economy has a contender, a substitute that is continually attempting to outshine the other. The most widely recognized reason for contests seen in such multi-item showcases is cost.

Normally customers are drawn to those things that have a lower cost of procurement than its substitute. Since there essentially exists separated items the general quality is pretty much something similar.

Now, from the producer's perspective, cutting costs is the only way to lower the price of his product. Be that as it may, techniques for creation can't be changed without changing the quality. Needless to say, if one must cut costs, quality will undoubtedly suffer as well. Increasing production scale would be another option. Yet, that is tedious. Thus, some other measure is expected for guaranteed impact.

Grocery stores and wholesalers utilize a normal strategy for evaluating, called block valuing. At the point when a shopper runs over a billboard that says, "Milk-1 gallon $3.00; 4 gallons for $10.00," he automatically makes the calculated observation that he is making some kind of gain by paying two dollars less for the bulk purchase.

Consequently, the job was well done. In spite of the fact that purchasing items in mass decreases the expense for the buyers clearly, his way of managing money would be unique assuming he had 1 gallon of milk available to him rather than 4 all at once.

One more method for catching the purchaser's eye is to give canny offers. The concept of FREE is well-known to everyone. It's a short word, yet it can do enormous things. Typically, one purchases conditioners with shampoos, cleans with cleansers and socks with shoes. In this way, if by purchasing a major container of cleanser one gets a little jug of conditioner FREE with it, then, at that point, that could draw in numerous purchasers.

Buffets at diners charge a proper cost for each head for dinners. This implies that the individual eating soup, Chicken a la Kiev and pastry pays equivalent to the individual eating just the chicken and sweet. This might sound out of line to individual 1, yet after all nobody wouldn't serve him soup.
Hence, in spite of the fact that cost is a variable, it is fundamentally a mental fight where the client is defined with numerous choices to browse.

Estimating an item based on its worth judgment is critical. Client inclinations, item benefits, organization picture, accommodation and item quality are abstract models that will assist an association with grasping the client's impression of the worth of its item or administration.
What clients need is imperative.

Is it true that they are setting aside cash or time by buying your item? If they use your service, do they gain a competitive advantage? What are their decisions? Is it advantageous for them to utilize your administration as opposed to doing it without anyone else's help? What precisely does the opposition interest?

The most extreme value the client will pay for the advantage can be perceived in the event that the above focuses are remembered.

Recorded underneath are a couple of significant worth based valuing systems. They take into account the break-even point, but in addition to the numbers, they include subjective opinions.

Laying out similar costs as contenders - This is involved when costs for an item are generally deep rooted (like proficient administrations), or when there could be no different means to set costs. The test, in this manner, is to sort out some way to bring down costs to create higher benefits when contrasted with contenders.

Laying out a Low Cost - This is done exclusively to catch an enormous number of clients in the market concerned. This technique is likewise used to acquire non-monetary goals like gathering the opposition, extending a picture of being minimal expense, or just for item mindfulness. On the off chance that productivity can be kept up with at the low cost, or on the other hand assuming deal levels are OK, this procedure works and can later prompt the raising of costs.

Charging an exorbitant cost - It is feasible to charge an excessive cost comparative with the expense of the item in the event that it is novel and is important to clients. The abundance of the objective market likewise counts. Situating an item as a "esteem item" in such a case would make it conceivable to charge an exorbitant cost. For instance, Rolex watches might not have that high a creation cost. Nonetheless, the excessive cost brings a "status" advantage to the well-off Rolex market.

Charging the clients what they "will pay", despite the fact that it is high, is a technique that requires sharpness and knowledge. It likewise requires a readiness to change since clients (as well as contenders) could conclude that the benefits are excessively high. Consequently, a great deal of elements impact esteem based evaluation, however an insightful planner can capitalize on it.

On the off chance that your costs are somewhat flawed you won't go anywhere regardless of whether you have the best item/administration on the planet. Web firms utilize three essential valuing systems POPS, Covers AND CAPS. They can only aid the companies in gaining an advantage over the rest if implemented correctly.

(POPS) PHYSICAL OBJECT PRICING STRATEGY, which sells a physical item and ships it to customers, is effective. Amazon.com and Wall-Shop fall under this classification. These organizations start at the base level to decide the cost by figuring out the amount it expenses to create and to convey one extra unit. (It is a negligible expense).

Let's take Wall-Mart as an illustration. They sell microwaves. How much would it cost them to sell an additional unit? To have to sort this out they would need to figure out the expense at which they purchase from their providers, cost at which they put it in the store and the expense at which they execute their exchange. So to decide the last value a firm needs to add to the minor expense.

The operating profit margin is as follows:

To figure out the rate they need to compare it and comparable different firms. Amazon has a 6% benefit. Contending retailers ought to focus on a similar working edge ideally a lower one would get the job done. A firm fostering a productive business cycle could limit their expenses and assist them with keeping their costs low while still holding their appealing edge.

(Covers) COST OF Procurement Estimating Technique. POPS functions admirably assuming your essential expense is the expense of the real expense of goods that you are conveying. In any case, firms that are selling item/administration where the expense is promoting based, related with the quantity of guests to your sight it might benefit by using Covers to decide their last cost. Covers typically address two key inquiries.

What will cost it to get individuals to visit a site?

What is the level of the site guests that could make the last buy?

The response of the primary inquiry ought to be isolated by the response of the second inquiry to give the firm its expense per obtaining. Therefore, the final price can be determined by adding the operating profit margin to this.

For instance a retailer might find that on a typical it costs 0.10$ for a the guest site and there might be 1% guests that make the buy. Thus, we simply derive the cost per acquisition from this point. Also, we figure out what ought to be the last cost. The key here is to limit the expense per obtaining.

(VAPS) Worth ADDED Valuing System. For organizations in which the negligible expense is no for instance in the offer of computerized items like digital books and online courses. VAPS work best while making a plan of action in which you can charge different costs to various clients.

www.ingramcontent.com/pod-product-compliance
Lightning Source LLC
Chambersburg PA
CBHW071010260726
48661CB00007B/2870